Organization
Technology
Culture

A playbook for implementing and maximizing the value of CRM

Jan Ropponen

Copyright
©Jan Ropponen

This book may not be lent, resold, hired out or otherwise disposed of by way of trade in any form of binding or cover other than that which it is published, without the prior consent of the Publisher. Neither the publisher nor the author make any legal representation or warranty with respect to the contents of the book, and they do not accept liability for any inaccuracy in the material in the book.

Table of contents

About the author 4
Introduction 6
Part 1 - Define 12
   Define your financial goals 12
   Objectives 14
   What needs to change? 16
      1. Increasing customer focus 17
      2. Improving sales management 19
      3. Increasing sales rep productivity 23
   Crafting your CRM vision 25
   Tying objectives to the needed CRM capabilities 26
   Define checklist 29
Part 2 - Plan 31
   Getting management and sales managers ready for change
.... 31
   Create measurable milestones 36
   Communicate early 39
   Plan checklist 40
Part 3 - Activate 42
   Activate through sales training and coaching - not CRM
training 43
   Strategic value checkpoints 46
   Building sustainable habits of world-class sales
organizations 47
   Activate checklist 50
Summary 52
Define, plan, and active Canvas 55

Sources 58

About the author

Sales transformation is more important than ever. Increasing pressure from competitors on a global scale, commoditization of products and services, as well as professional purchasing is squeezing the profits and growth efforts of most B2B companies. Modernizing the B2B operating model, developing sales skills faster and leveraging technology are all keys to increasing results.

Jan Ropponen helps B2B companies plan and execute successful sales transformations. Working with many different companies in the past years, Jan has observed how a lot of companies see technology as a magic wand that will solve their problems. For example, many companies invest in a CRM that they believe will automatically give them the visibility they need to steer their sales operations and improve their forecasting. Another example is that companies implement marketing automation that will start creating leads by itself and improve sales cycles. Both CRM and marketing automation are great opportunities, but require change in how sales is managed and how the sales organization works on a daily basis.

Technology can do wonderful things, but not by itself. Jan is on a mission to help companies make the necessary changes to fully leverage the power of technology.

Introduction

The speed at which the economy runs these days, combined with the super intensive competitive situation means that companies without superior commercial execution will not make it in this marketplace. By superior commercial execution, we mean the speed and efficiency of creating revenue through the means of sales and marketing. Simply stated: obtaining more customers and growing existing customers.

So what are the core elements of superior commercial execution? We believe there are two key things that differentiate the superior from the mediocre.

Number one: Sales management

Number two: CRM technology and its proper adoption

No matter how great the CRM is, without great sales management it is essentially a worthless CRM. This is a 1+1=3 equation. Great sales management combined with a CRM is the key to superior sales execution which leads to above average results. For the best organizations, CRM has become much more than a tool used by sales reps. These superior organizations have completely integrated CRM with their way of working and operating model. It has become the backbone of their sales, marketing and service organizations.

"High-performing sales teams use nearly 3 times as much sales technology than underperforming teams and are 8 times more likely to be heavy tech adopters than underperformers." (1)

Unfortunately, many organizations use their CRM merely as a reporting tool, mostly used by sales reps for management reporting purposes. In these cases adoption levels are often low. The CRM data is not real-time and dependable, so executives and sales management do not trust the information, and therefore decisions and coaching cannot be based on the CRM data. It's a death spiral. The information is not dependable, so the system is not that important, and therefore salespeople use the system even less.

We see a huge gap between high-performers and the rest, and how they are using CRM.

The goal of this book is to help you fill this gap and bring your performance up to a level where you can beat the competition and reach your full potential.

CRM in the context of this book is the platform that you are using to manage and execute customer facing activities. It's a system that automates the manual tasks that the best sales reps used to do on paper, and it gives the sales organization the needed visibility to be managed. If implemented correctly, CRM is the platform that enables you to sell more.

CRM is of high-importance, but many still fail in their implementation efforts

Many studies show that over 50% of CRM implementations fail. For example, Merkle Group interviewed over 300 US based executives, and found that 63% of these executives considered that their CRM implementations had failed. (2)

There are numerous reasons for this which will be covered in this book.

This book does not have a technology focus as we do not believe that these failure rates have much to do with the technology itself. We will focus on what needs to happen in order to align your organization to reaching your strategic targets. CRM is not about technology, it is a philosophy and a sales organizational discipline. This philosophy and discipline is at the core of world-class sales organizations today.

Who is this book for?

Whether you are planning on implementing, or have already implemented your CRM, this book is for you if you want to raise your organization's performance by using CRM properly.

This book could have been 10 times longer, but we know you are busy so we wanted to keep this playbook simple, yet include the absolutely most important things to help guide your change management efforts. This is a book that is both easy to read and use as a workbook in leading your change efforts.

Although a modern CRM in a B2B context is much broader than only a platform for the sales organization, in this book we will focus on bringing the sales organization up to full speed by implementing the CRM properly. The principles can be applied to any type of CRM implementation, including bringing marketing, service, field service and partners onto your CRM.

What CRM was 15 years ago is radically different than from today. CRM was a tool for salespeople, now it is a platform for the whole organization to engage with customers. At its best the CRM platform is also extended as a platform for partners and customers where they can get insights into relevant information and data.

Three steps to success - Define, plan and activate

This book has been divided into three different parts.

1. Define

The first part helps define what success is going to look like by turning strategic goals into priorities and then further turning these priorities into needed capabilities. When these capabilities are used, the value of changing needs to be defined by numbers and we need to define the financial impact that we're looking to achieve. CRM is always an investment, mostly in your time put towards changing. As everything else in business, this investment needs to have a payoff.

2. Plan

The second part is about making sure that needed financial impact is reached.

Who do we need to involve and how do we split this sales transformation project into smaller bite size steps to ensure that we succeed?

3. Activate

The third and last part focuses on getting the whole organization involved and succeeding in making the necessary change happen in a sustainable way.

In this part we focus on how the changes that you implement become habits that enable consistent commercial execution.

Checklists

There is a checklist at the end of each section of this book. The checklists are for you to ensure everything that was covered in the chapter is in good shape on your behalf. You can use them to track your progress for each task that must be done.

Use the checklists to give yourself a grade and make an honest evaluation on how ready you are to make the necessary changes.

Part 1 - Define

Define your financial goals

When done right, your CRM should become a competitive advantage for you in the market you compete in. Before going deeper into this section of the book, let's take a step back and look at the market that you're competing in. You need to have a solid understanding of the goals you must reach and how your are developing your competitive advantage.

Here are some questions to get you started:

- How do you define the market(s) you are competing in?
- What position do you want to achieve in this market?
- Do you want to grow faster than the market?
- Are you looking to grow revenue or is profitability your main focus at the moment?
- Are you going to be launching new product lines or changing your business model?
- How much of your revenue is going to come through your external channels and how much revenue will your field sales generate?
- What are your competitors doing and how are you planning on beating them?
- Where do you foresee that your profits will be coming from in 5 years?

- Are you willing to sacrifice short-term profits for improved long-term growth?

The answers to these questions are very relevant when choosing and implementing a CRM. It's good to remember that choosing and implementing a CRM from a technical standpoint is only a small part of your CRM implementation. The larger and more difficult part of this CRM project will be on how you change your ways of working and adopt new processes that everyone will work by. In order to reach your financial goals, you will be changing how you manage customers, how you lead sales and how your sales reps manage their daily tasks.

Another good reason to have very clear goals is that developing a business is just like politics. Your budgets and time are finite resources, so a clear focus and well defined strategic goals must guide us in your decision making and development initiatives.

You need to have a very compelling reason to change and create a movement that will enable the whole organization to start working in new ways.

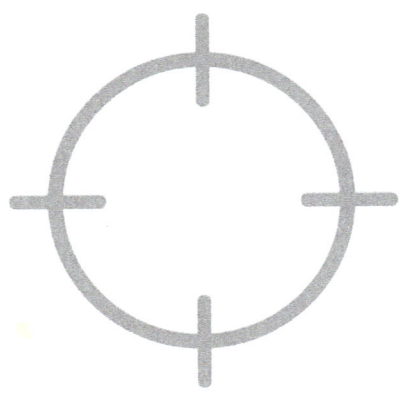

Objectives

Now that you have a clear picture of your strategic goals, how are you going to achieve them? What are the barriers and risks that prevent you from reaching your goals?

Some like to call these *top priorities* or *must win battles*. Whatever you choose to call them they need to be clearly defined.

Let's say your strategic goal is to double the size of your company from 100M $ to 200M $.

Will growth come from your current customers or do you need to acquire more customers? Are these new geographical areas or new product and service segments?

In this case your three objectives could be:

Objective #1 Acquire new customers

Objective #2 Grow current customer

Objective #3 Develop new product offering & create new revenue streams

Splitting your objectives into KPI's

Your KPI's will be your guiding compasses along the way. They will show you that the changes you are making are working, as long as they are properly aligned with your objectives.

Here are some examples of KPI's that help you reach your objectives:

- Existing business pipeline
- Current business pipeline
- Average annual revenue per customer / per segment
- Average deal size
- Leads per month
- Win-rate (not the best in all industries or situations - but a highly used KPI)
- Sales cycle (time from opportunity creation to opportunity close)

Less is always more with KPI's. Having 3-5 KPI's per objective is a sufficient amount.

What needs to change?

What needs to change in order for you to reach your objectives?

The most important question we need to answer now is: Why aren't you reaching your goals with your current organization and processes?

Sometimes the answer could be "we are not 100% sure". This is an acceptable answer if you don't have a CRM properly in use. If you had a CRM and it was in full use, you could answer this question as you would have access to data and be able to look at it from any dimension you would like to.

Most likely reaching your strategic goals will need improvement and investments in other areas outside your sales and marketing activities. This playbook focuses on what you as a sales professional can have an impact on, which is is how well you execute the strategy. Your actions have a major impact on objectives # 1 and #2.

The different areas that you can focus on in order to reach your objectives are split into three themes.

1. Increasing customer focus - "We need to become more customer focused"

2. Improving sales management - "We need to steer our sales efforts and investments smarter"
3. Increasing sales rep productivity - "We need to work smarter and spend more time selling"

1. Increasing customer focus

Most CRM projects should focus exactly on what the definition of CRM is, Customer Relationship Management. So how serious are you really about your customers? Do you want to put them at the center of everything you do?

Creating a customer centric culture is key to a successful CRM implementation. Since many different people within your company are working with the same customers, there is a huge amount of benefits in getting the whole company to huddle around your customers.

A traditional CRM was a tool only for salespeople who were the only customer facing employees. Nowadays things have changed, and there are usually several people in the organization engaging with the same customer. New CRM platforms such as Salesforce.com differ in a major way from other vendors, because it's not only a tool, but more of a business ecosystem that allows your whole organization to fully align with your customers. This means that in addition to salespeople, also marketing, back-office and upper management are using the platform, with everyone having a 360 view of your customer relationships. At its best your CRM can also extend to your customers and channel partners via a community that sits on top of your CRM, so that you can share beneficial data with your customers and partners.

How will an increase in customer focus impact customers?

- Fast and more consistent service
- Buying becomes so easy that customers don't want to buy from others than you
- No lost information - whoever the customer talks to, the person understands them
- Customers receive the level of service they pay for - Different customer segments will have different approaches if you have a segmented approach.
- Seamless cooperation between marketing and sales departments means that the marketing communication that customers receive are highly relevant and beneficial for the customer
- With more focus on the customer, the sales process will be more customer centric and make buying easier for customers

Create a single version of the truth if you want to be customer centric

Many companies cannot simply operate in a customer centric way because their data is all over the place. It's in the notebooks and calendars of salespeople and sales managers. It's in spreadsheets and different documents that only salespeople have access to. The data could also be spread across multiple systems.

The data that the sales team is creating can be used by the whole organization to steer the business in benefit of the customers. R&D, production, marketing, logistics, and top management all benefit from the information that is produced on a daily basis.

Huddling the whole company around your customers, allows you to operate in a unified way. This is the ultimate goal of a CRM implementation. If this is a core part of your implementation, then you are on the right way. Keep pushing forward.

It doesn't matter how much a company wants to become customer centric if there is not a central place for a 360 view of the customer!

2. Improving sales management

Running a top-performing sales organization is becoming more of a science, and less of an art. Without full visibility into the sales operations, there is no way for sales management to know where to begin improving the results.

How sales management uses the CRM as a part of their sales management routines is crucial. Front-line sales managers have a crucial role in pushing and enabling salespeople to use the system. Without full adoption there will be no data.

And without data it will be very hard to manage a sales organization and coach the sales people to success. Remember: adoption before data!

CRM is more than order data and customer information

The problem with order data, is that you have no forward view of the business. Enterprise resource planning (ERP) and financial systems tell you what has happened, not what is going to happen. The CRM is your execution system for what will happen. If you don't have a clue of what the future looks like it becomes extremely difficult to steer the business. Are you set up to succeed or are you going to miss our targets? Without a CRM in proper use steering and forecasting will be very hard for you.

Here are some questions that sit well into the sales management category

- How well are you able to forecast at the moment?
- How well can you spot trends that are happening in the market?
- How easy is it to set goals, and plan sales activities?
- How can you coach salespeople with the data you have on their activities?
- Would there be major benefits in steering the business in real-time? Are you able to recognize trends and changes in the marketplace faster than your competitors?
- Would you benefit from splitting and segmenting your sales data in any way you like to?
- Are you able to see your full funnel at the moment? All leads and opportunities in the funnel?

How well does the sales management in your organization perform in these three areas that they are responsible for?

1. **Set goals**

- Align company strategy with sales goals
- Set team goals
- Enage sales reps to set ambitious goals

2. **Plan**

- Align goals with the right metrics to guide activity
- Set territory plans
- Set account plans
- Decide on marketing actions to fully support sales

3. **Execute**

- Coach activity, not results
- Coach with CRM dashboards
- Motivate
- Optimize marketing and sales alignment activities continuously

Would you say that management is capable of doing the above? How well do your current systems help to perform these activities?

This is a good check list, as sales managers should be able to do all of the above better with the help of your CRM platform. You can use this as a checklist for reflecting on your strengths and weaknesses, and think of what needs to be developed.

3. Increasing sales rep productivity

By productivity we mainly mean the results that one sales person can achieve per unit of their time. For example, output per day of work. Simplifying and streamlining the way salespeople work on one platform can create enormous gains in efficiency. Add automation to this and we have even further gains.

So productivity is one important area, but a CRM should be much more than only a productivity booster. A CRM should help with scaling best practices and streamlining the way your company works. The CRM should guide the sales people along the identified best ways of working to help customers reach a "yes" decision. The CRM should help your entire sales organization to follow a process that makes them better salespeople.

"Good management consists in showing average people how to do the work of superior people"

-John D. Rockefeller

A few questions to determine your situation:

- How much more do you think your sales reps could sell if they increased their productivity by lets say 20%?
- How much smarter do you think they could sell and what exactly would smarter mean for your sales reps?

Combining coaching with CRM

One ultimate goal of a sales manager should be to develop self guided sales reps. Using dashboards in the CRM during coaching and sales meetings, should lead to a situation where after a while, sales reps can diagnose their own situation and what they should do to sell more. This is the outcome of solid continuous coaching!

If sales reps aren't using dashboards on their own, they will have little incentive to make sure they are using the system properly every day.

Align sales and marketing

If salespeople receive the support of marketing in creating demand in their territories and having a constant flow of leads, that's already a big reason to use the CRM properly. Aligning the actions of sales and marketing should be one major area that makes salespeople more productive, as they are able to focus on high value work and marketing can focus on scalable marketing initiatives.

Crafting your CRM vision

The importance of creating a clear vision for what you are going to achieve can't be understated. A clear vision based on your strategic goals makes it easier to communicate the necessary change needed. It should get everyone aligned with why the CRM implementation is so crucial.

I've worked with customers that want to become the best sales organization in their industry and crush the competition. They are extremely motivated and want to be the #1 in their industry and they understand that the way they have been working previously must change. Everyone wants to be a part of a winning team! We hope you do to.

We will not set any specific guidelines for what a CRM vision should include. We do however, recommend that it includes at least your goal, and how your CRM will help you reach that goal. The most important thing is that your CRM vision must help you articulate what you want to achieve by implementing a new system and new ways of working.

Your CRM vision could include the following:
- Becoming the most customer obsessed company in your industry
- Becoming the market leader
- Having the most satisfied customers
- Working as ONE company
- Becoming a strategic partner for customers
- Helping your customers throughout their whole lifecycle

Tying objectives to the needed CRM capabilities

Now that we have defined your financial goals and identified the areas that you need to change and the KPI's, it-much easier to zoom in on the capabilities that you need from your CRM. These capabilities will enable you to make the necessary changes in behavior and company processes.

Changing the operating model could for example be that our sales reps take care of too much of the customer lifecycle, and therefore do not have enough time to sell. They take care of everything from start to finish. In this case, moving to a more focused sales organization with specific responsibilities is a good move, which is already the modus operandi in all essentially fast growing sales organizations.

Sales development representatives prospect and fill the pipeline together with marketing, while field sales is out closing deals. In this model, several salespeople work with the same customers during their lifecycle. Marketing, service and customer success also need to be aligned to help the sales reps grow these customers.

In this type of set-up, everyone needs to have access to the same information and work together. That is why the CRM platform will be absolutely crucial if you want to reorganize in this way.

Here are some examples of features that enable solving the challenges described above.

Increased visibility for management to steer the business:

- Company dashboards
- Team dashboards
- Individual dashboards

Sales rep productivity features:

- Improved up-selling and cross-selling - whitespace analysis, analytics of the business

- Advanced CPQ tools for salespeople to configure the right solution and bundling for the customer, price it and send a quote
- Sales enablement - guide sales people to success
    - Groups to share best practices
    - Opportunity paths with best practices at each opportunity stage
    - Opportunity playbooks & templates in your CRM
- Automatically capturing activity - saving time from manually logging activities
- Automate manual tasks: reminders, next steps, tasks, lead follow up,
    - For example whenever you create an opportunity over 100K, your manager knows. If a contract is ending, 120 days before the sales person gets a task to be in touch or if a key account hasn't made an order in 6 months, notify the account owner.
- Account plans - One place to plan and execute actions for key accounts
- Improve customer engagements - meeting feedback app

Below you will find a simplified sketch for you to use for connecting your goals to the needed capabilities. The capabilities are functionalities of the system that enable your organization to work in the ways that will allow you to reach your goals.

The key is to have a logic chain of events, that you can link to each other.

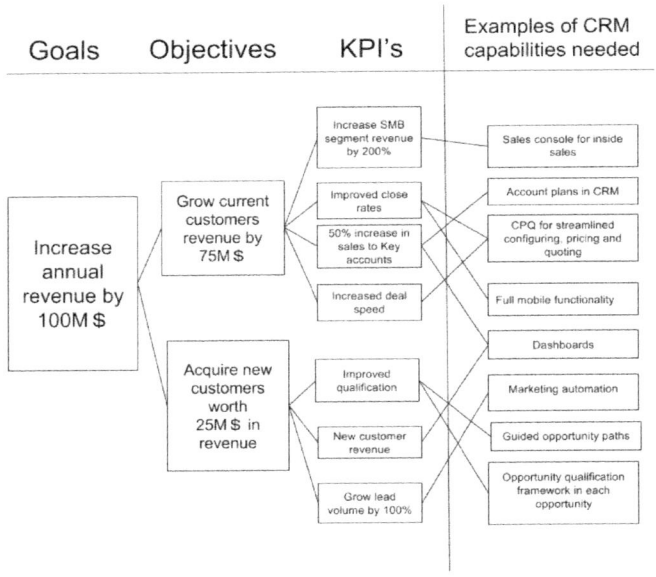

Define checklist

Task	Definition	Grade: 0-10	Action points
Strategic goals	What are your strategic goals for the coming 1-5 years?		
Top priorities	What are your top priorities that you are focusing on in order to reach your strategic goals?		
What needs to change?	What must you change in your sales execution in order to reach your goals?		
CRM Vision	What is the compelling reason for getting a new CRM and what will it accomplish?		
Capabilities tied to goals	How clearly can you define the capabilities that you are lacking at the moment in order to achieve your strategic targets?		

Part 2 - Plan

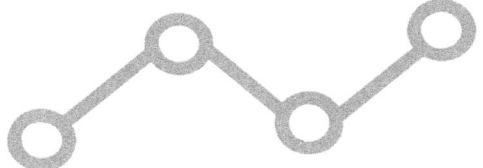

Getting management and sales managers ready for change

> *"Values and behavioral norms are simply not transmitted easily by talk or memo, but are conveyed very effective by doing and doing visibly."*
>
> Andy Grove, Former legendary CEO of Intel

The name of this book is *Organization, technology and culture* for a reason. Without the proper culture, the organization will not reach its full potential, even if it is enabled by state-of-the-art technology.

We always want to be careful with assumptions, but it should be safe to assume that in most organizations, there is plenty of management engagement and involvement in what was covered in part 1 of the book, which covered setting your strategic goals and objectives.

Management involvement should not end here, as the change project and CRM implementation proceeds to further stages. We need management to be involved in the planning (Part 2) and active stages (Part 3) as well.

If we only focus on implementing the CRM for sales reps to use and just focus on training them to be able to use the system, it will not become an organization wide change effort. Management and managers will not be involved enough, and this is the reason why many efforts to implement CRM fail.

In the picture below, we've scaled the weight of importance regarding training end users and creating an organization-wide change in habits and culture.

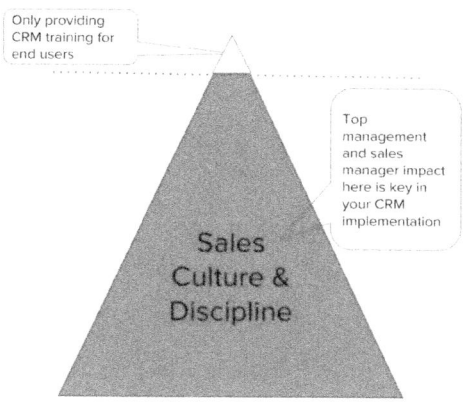

If you only provide training, it's just the tip of the iceberg. It will not make any lasting change in the way you operate.

A winning sales culture

A winning sales culture is such a strong force, that once it is built, nothing can stop it. This type of sales culture is defined and built at the top with management. That is why we know that this element will make it or break it for your organization, depending on how involved and how much ownership management has taken.

CRM is a philosophy of putting the customer in the center

CRM is not only a technology platform, it is a philosophy and a culture change for an organization that wants to reach its full potential. The way you do business and how you put the customers in the center of your business is core to reaping CRM benefits. This type of customer centricity and focus has to be set at the top and made into an organization wide initiative.

Imagine the impact a CEO or leader can make when sales reps see their comments on their own or others won deals, or if management is cheering on sales people after a great quarter.

Sales managers are the true heroes of change

When we look at how the sales strategy is executed, the sales managers are crucial. If the sales managers are not 100% convinced that the new CRM will enable you to sell faster and smarter, their poor attitude and lack of belief will poison the whole sales organization. These sales managers are the most important advocates for forming the right daily and weekly habits for the salespeople in the organization.

Management and managers need to be involved and excited if you want to succeed at implementing a CRM. That's the bottom line!

CRM ownership

Now that we have management and managers on board, we need to have a clear owner for the CRM. Depending on the size of your business and your organizational model your ownership set-up will be different. In many organizations IT will have ownership of all IT-applications. Our advice here is that since your CRM is the backbone of your commercial execution, as much ownership as possible should be taken by the sales organization. Progress and ownership should be in the hands of the sales organization at least the first 6-12 months after the initial implementation.

A few words on data

Your mentality must be that your data is either terrible or it's great. Even if your data is in 80% good shape, you can't trust it. Would you trust a person who lies to you 20% of the time? We sure wouldn't and we hope you don't either.

As Yoda says, "Do or do not, there is no try". Managers set the culture and standards that will determine how good your data is. A deep commitment is needed to reach the right level of discipline.

What is good to note is that your must strive for perfection, but your data will never be 100% correct. Situations change and some things require manual updates. External data about customers is constantly changing and will never be 100% up to date, but should always be as close as possible to 100%. If you do not strive for perfection, than the data quality will not be satisfactory. Internal data concerning order start and end dates, or delivery terms are a different story. This type of information can't have any flaws, and a small error in your process could lead to hundreds of dissatisfied customers every year.

Create measurable milestones

A big change can be quite challenging with hundreds of elements and people involved, so even mentally picturing the change can be difficult. Once this is split to a micro level, the change is quite manageable and easy to understand. Your milestones will link your vision to concrete small steps that will carry you towards reaching that vision.

Your milestones will serve as quick wins, on a weekly, biweekly or monthly level!

By measurable milestones we mean the kind of features and functionality that will be delivered, and more importantly how your sales organization's routines and processes will change along with utilizing that functionality.

Now that you have your strategic targets set in stone, you are able to split them into smaller objectives and metrics, which will allow you to zoom in closer on the daily actions that need to happen. Big targets are hard to hit, but I'm sure you can hit 24 smaller smaller targets, when you focus on hitting one at a time.

Here is an example of some milestones that can been included in delivery plans.

Milestone	Date	Metrics
Successful training	Week 1	Salespeople have "seen the light" and have understood how the CRM helps them - They are able to technically use the system
Activities being used: meetings, calls	Week 2	Sales reps activity can be seen holistically from your team dashboards.
Adoption 100%	Week 3	Login rate & login leader board. Sales reps are using

		the CRM every day.
All leads are visible in the system	Week 4	Leads and lead status is visible on lead level and on a dashboard as a whole
Pipeline always 100% up to date	Week 5	No need to update anything in meetings
CRM is used in mobile devices	Week 6	Everyone has accessed and uses mobile CRM on a daily level
Using collaboration within the CRM for all sales related discussions, especially everything that is related to Accounts, contacts and opportunities	Week 7	E-mail not used for discussing opportunities or other sales related topics
Next steps always visible in the CRM for key accounts	Week 8	Every opportunity has clearly defined next steps Every opportunity past a certain stage has a clearly defined visible plan for how the opportunity will be won
The CRM is never "updated", it is a real-time platform that all sales reps use for their daily sales activities ("reporting" is not needed, information is always accurate)	Week 9	In sales meetings, does anything need to be updated or not? When sales managers coach salespeople, do you have all the data you need to understand what they are doing so you can guide them to improve

		performance?
Sales management has the needed visibility to be able to make decisions and also coach sales reps	Week 10	Do sales managers have the CRM open in sales meetings and do they navigate the discussions using the dashboards and reports to steer the discussion? If you need to look deeper and talk about a specific opportunity, do you open up the opportunity in the system and use the visible information as the foundation for the discussion?
Spreadsheets are not being used any more	Week 11	All activity and deal tracking is done through the CRM
Account plans in CRM	Week 12	Can you see what actions have been planned for a specific customers and what the goals for the customer are? Can you compare the plan vs. how the account plan is being executed? Are we on track to reaching the sales goals for this specific account?

Communicate early

Just like leadership and change management in general, communication is key. Nobody likes surprises and everyone wants to be heard.

If you know about the coming changes a year in advance, you should start communicating about it right way. The best alternative is to involve as many as possible as early as possible. So ask for feedback and engage the organization. It's incredible what kind of insight can be derived from this type of open change management.

Right from the beginning, the entire organizations needs should to be considered so you know the answer to these questions: What's in it for each salesperson? How will it make their lives easier?

Focus on why the change is necessary and what the potential gain is for the individuals. By building a vision early, it becomes easy to start communicating and developing the vision.

Plan checklist

Task	Definition	Grade: 0-10	Action points
Management on board	Do you have a C-level sponsor who is going to be involved in this project? Do you have sales management actively involved in every step of the way in your delivery plan with measurable milestones?		
Sales managers on board	Are the sales managers who lead the front-line salespeople 100% convinced that this new change is good and will help you succeed and make their lives easier?		
Create measurable milestones	Have you been able to define the steps along the way to reaching 100% CRM implementation success?		
Communicate early	How will you communicate about the urgency and necessity of the coming changes way in advance to prepare the organization?		

Part 3 - Activate

"We are what we repeatedly do. Excellence, then, is not an act, but a habit."
                                                    -Aristotle

True professionals, whether it be in sports or business, know that success is all about habits and attention to detail. This is exactly what sales excellence is all about. It is not an act, but a habit and a continuous discipline. That's what sets amateurs and top professionals apart.

This third part of the book is about making the necessary changes to build winning habits, that ultimately are the key to maximizing your results.

In the first stage (Define) we defined the goals you need to reach, and the capabilities that will enable you to reach the goals. This third part is where the magic will happen, because here we are making the needed changes happen and changing the culture and your ways of working.

Never underestimate how much work this will take! Just remember, it's 100% worth it. No pain, no gain.

Activate through sales training and coaching - not CRM training

One of the biggest mistakes we see happening is that a company hires a technical CRM consultant to set up the system, and then they also want the technical consultant to train everyone to use the system.

"The scenario we describe next is highly unrealistic: The consultant begins by asking for requirements, sets up the system, runs a few training sessions for the salespeople on how the system technically works, and voilà the CRM system is in full use by the whole organization! This is something that never happens, which is why you shouldn't try go there either. It could turn out to be a huge mistake and slow down your change efforts.

As described in the two previous parts in this book, there's a good reason we've got management and sales managers involved early. They are the ones who will help drive the necessary change, not an outside technical consultant!

How do you feed a dog its medication when it doesn't want to eat it?

Going to CRM training is like eating disgusting pills for salespeople. They don't all necessary love sales training either, but most would prefer going to a sales training that will help them succeed, rather than listening to an outsider that comes and tells them how the reporting system will work.

This is one reason for running CRM training as sales training instead. The key is to make it fun, interactive and make sure everyone learns how to sell better.

So if you do use consultants, they should be focused on coaching your salespeople and sales management to be better sales professionals and use the system as a part of the training in a natural way. When the person that runs the training really knows the business, and understands what happens in the day of a salesperson, the training approach can be run in a very high context for the salesperson and therefore the impact of the training will be much more powerful.

If sales managers are crucial to driving the necessary change, how can we make sure they are fully equipped with the right skills and knowledge?

The answer is: have the sales managers run the training sessions!

We should make sure that the sales managers who are operating the daily business with front-line salespeople have the skillsets needed to actually run the training. If they are capable of running the trainings and fully understand the system, they will feel comfortable leading their sales teams with this new platform.

It's not a bad idea to use outside help to accelerate the process of getting the managers and management fully up to speed with the CRM.

The training should be focused on your sales process (hopefully very customer centric), because everyone must understand why the sales process is designed the way it is. A special focus should be given to how the sales process and daily routines will change and why the change is good! This is everything we walked through in parts 1 and 2 of this book.

Driving the change will be easier when using your own customer cases and situations to demo and practice different sales scenarios. This is 10x better than simply showing how to use the system. Practice how to perform in everyday sales situations and use the system to do that. The focus will not be on the system, but the system will be in the background to help us run the sales process according to the new processes and habits.

If you have a sales playbook, this will probably be a good manual to use for the training, instead of a manual on how to use the CRM system by itself.

In summary, train management and sales managers first. Once they are fully on board, bring the sales people to join the movement!

Strategic value checkpoints

In part 1 we focused on defining strategic goals and financial targets to reach. Since these high level goals are something that should be a part of your everyday business, we don't suggest having a different follow-up procedure for those. What we do suggest is that you set a few checkpoints aside, where you will reflect on the specific impact of the changes you have made and documented, as we described in parts 1 and 2.

In these checkpoints you take a holistic look at what has been achieved, and what you still need to improve. The checkpoints ensure that the capabilities we were looking to develop have been achieved so that the strategic goals can be reached.

Set a few checkpoints for example for 6, 12 and 18 months after the go-live of the implementation. Look at your own version of the picture below for evaluation of how well you have succeeded.

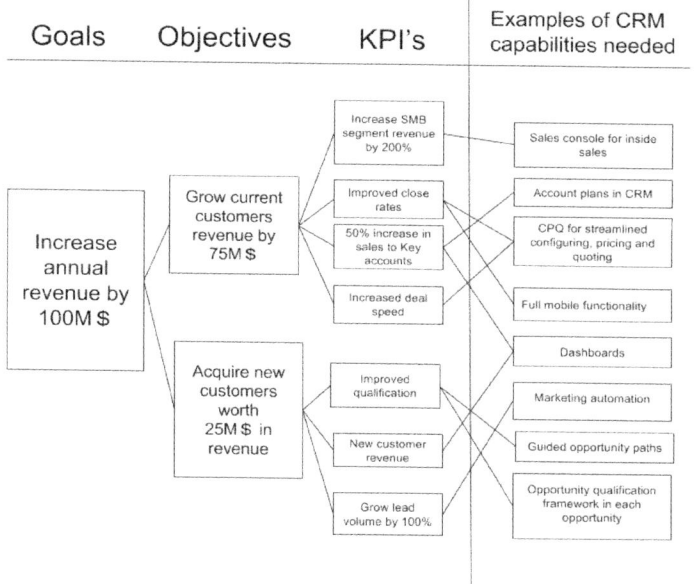

Building sustainable habits of world-class sales organizations

How fast do you have to make a first impression? Some say five seconds while others say a minute. Whatever you think the length could be, it's probably short.

The same goes for your CRM implementation. From the go-live date when users start using the system, they will begin forming those good or bad habits. It's up to the managers to make sure that they steer this ship in the right direction from the get go.

How fast habits can be changed, surely depends on the variation between what kind of habits we are trying to form. According to one the study, it takes 66 days to form a new habit. And by habit we mean tasks that can be performed automatically without having to do too much mental work. (3)

Creating success in the first 60 days

Our goal is to make the use of the CRM so natural, that it becomes automatic. We need to be able to shift our focus and all our energy on customers and selling to them as fast as possible, not on using the system.

That is why we must create new habits that stick and become natural. We need the new habits to be formed very quickly and plenty of reinforcement. We need to start changing the habits from day one.

If sales managers are not enforcing the necessary habits, within the first 60 days, then perhaps the new habits you were hoping to form will never be achieved.

For example, a very dangerous sentence that a sales manager can say is "it's OK, update your opportunities when you get the chance". These types of comments and lack of discipline are detrimental to your success.

Reaching the milestones described in part 2, will not be possible to reach without creating new habits.

Rules for creating new habits

We've found it easy to start creating new habits by having a document with clear guidelines for managers.

The key here is not to just create a document and hand it over to sales managers and expect them to start living by the rules. The rules must be created together. We cannot have a "not invented here" syndrome happen.

Here are some examples of things you can include in your rules for sales managers:

1. In meetings and coaching situations, always open up the CRM and walk through the session with the information in your CRM
2. Don't have a meeting and coach, if the information in your CRM is not up to date
3. Don't accept spreadsheets from salespeople
4. Don't accept updating the system in sales meetings

5. If a salesperson calls or asks for help about something that's not in the system, you will not help
6. If a salesperson emails you about an opportunity, do not answer the e-mail. Only answer if they use the collaboration tool in the CRM (This can feel cruel, but you must direct them towards discussing the opportunity openly within the CRM for transparency and ease of following up next time you talk about the opportunity)
7. Don't discuss an opportunity without next steps in the system (if the salesperson has next steps, but it's not seen in the system on the opportunity)
8. Do give praise and thanks to you sales reps for good work in a transparent manner in your CRM environment (In Salesforce this is Chatter)

Activate checklist

Task	Definition	Grade: 0-10	Action points
Activate through sales training & coaching	How will you provide sales training & coaching and use the CRM as a part of the training?		
Strategic value checkpoints	When will you review the impact of your change efforts and the CRM implementation?		
Winning habits defined	What are the specific habits that need to be embedded in your organization? Create some kind of commandments or rules to follow by.		

Summary

Looking back on successful CRM implementations, learning to use the software has always been the easiest part. It's the change that should come along with the system that is the hard part. Instead of thinking about a CRM implementation as one implementation, perhaps it would be more realistic to think of it this way: every individual is its own little implementation project. Every person has a different background, capability of changing their routines, and way of working (part 3). Because of this, what's really been key is getting people involved at every stage of the process, and making a company wide commitment to reach a common goal (part 1 and 2).

If you're not focusing enough on one part of the three, it will cause challenges down the road. We see many companies skipping part 2, and creating an implementation plan from only a very technical perspective, without planning on how the organization and culture will be changed. We hope this book will serve you as a workbook to not only help with one implementation, but something that can help drive any change initiatives. CRM isn't one big implementation anymore , but rather a series of continuous improvements. Every improvement is a change in some type of process and behavior. All three parts of this book will be present in almost any change that needs to happen in your organization.

Up until now, some businesses have been able to get away without fully succeeding in their CRM implementations. As we are moving into the age of artificial intelligence, the basics of data management in your CRM will be exponentially important. The CRM is linked to everything, and is actually your business ecosystem that allows you to collaborate with customers and partners.

Because of its business critical role, a failure in a CRM implementation is not a failure of adopting a sales tool, but a failure in a business critical project that could be detrimental to your business. That's why it's better to focus on getting the basics right and creating sales disciplines and approaches that differentiate you in your market. Your CRM is your execution platform for this.

The partnership that needs to be built between people and technology is achieved by focusing on people.

Put your people first!

Define, plan, and active Canvas

Define	
Strategic goals	
Top priorities	
Change needed	
CRM capabilities needed	
Plan	
Management on board the project	
Change plan with milestones	
Activate	
Activate through sales training	
Daily habits rules created	

Sources

1. Salesforce State of Sales report - Salesforce research
https://secure.sfdcstatic.com/assets/pdf/misc/state-of-sales-report-salesforce.pdf

2. 63% of CRM initiatives fail - Merkle Group, Jonathan Prezant - July 17, 2013
https://www.merkleinc.com/thought-leadership/feature-articles/marketing-solutions-and-strategies/customer-strategy/63-crm-initiatives-fail

3. How long does it take to form a habit? - UCL Epidemiology and Public Health
http://www.ucl.ac.uk/news/news-articles/0908/09080401

Yes this is not about a study of business habits specifically. We believe our basic human instincts are formed in the same way whether its routines at work or home at the dinner table.

Printed in Great Britain
by Amazon

47021101R00037